# Contents

*This is a progressive course. Start with Step 1.*
*Make sure you can play each step before moving on to the next.*

| | |
|---|---|
| Are you sitting comfortably? . . . . . . . . . . . . . 2 | Musical terms . . . . . . . . . . . . . . . . . . . . . . 7 |
| Why **No Notes**? . . . . . . . . . . . . . . . . . . . . 3 | Acknowledgements . . . . . . . . . . . . . . . . . 24 |
| Getting started . . . . . . . . . . . . . . . . . . . . . . 4 | Foundation keyboard skills . . . . . *inside back cover* |
| Practice hints . . . . . . . . . . . . . . . . . . . . . . . 6 | |

| | | | | |
|---|---|---|---|---|
| Step 1. | Learning to walk . . . . . . . . . . . 8 | Step 9. | Blues Scale Blues . . . . . . . . . . . 16 |
| Step 2. | Shuffle Riff . . . . . . . . . . . . . . . 9 | Step 10. | Syncopated Rhythm . . . . . . . . . 17 |
| Step 3. | Playing with a beat . . . . . . . . . 10 | Step 11. | Syncopated Groove . . . . . . . . . 18 |
| Step 4. | Backbeat Groove . . . . . . . . . . 11 | Step 12. | Syncopated Groove Blues . . . . . . . . 19 |
| Step 5. | Chords 1, 4 and 5 . . . . . . . . . . 12 | Step 13. | Syncopated Riff . . . . . . . . . . . 20 |
| Step 6. | 12-bar blues . . . . . . . . . . . . . 13 | Step 14. | Turnarounds . . . . . . . . . . . . . 21 |
| Step 7. | The blues scale . . . . . . . . . . . 14 | Step 15. | Straight 8s and swing . . . . . . . . . . 22 |
| Step 8. | Using the blues scale – 'inversions' . . . . 15 | Step 16. | Playing the blues . . . . . . . . . . . 23 |

**Free recordings of all No Notes music are available from www.NoNotes.co.uk**

# Are you sitting comfortably?

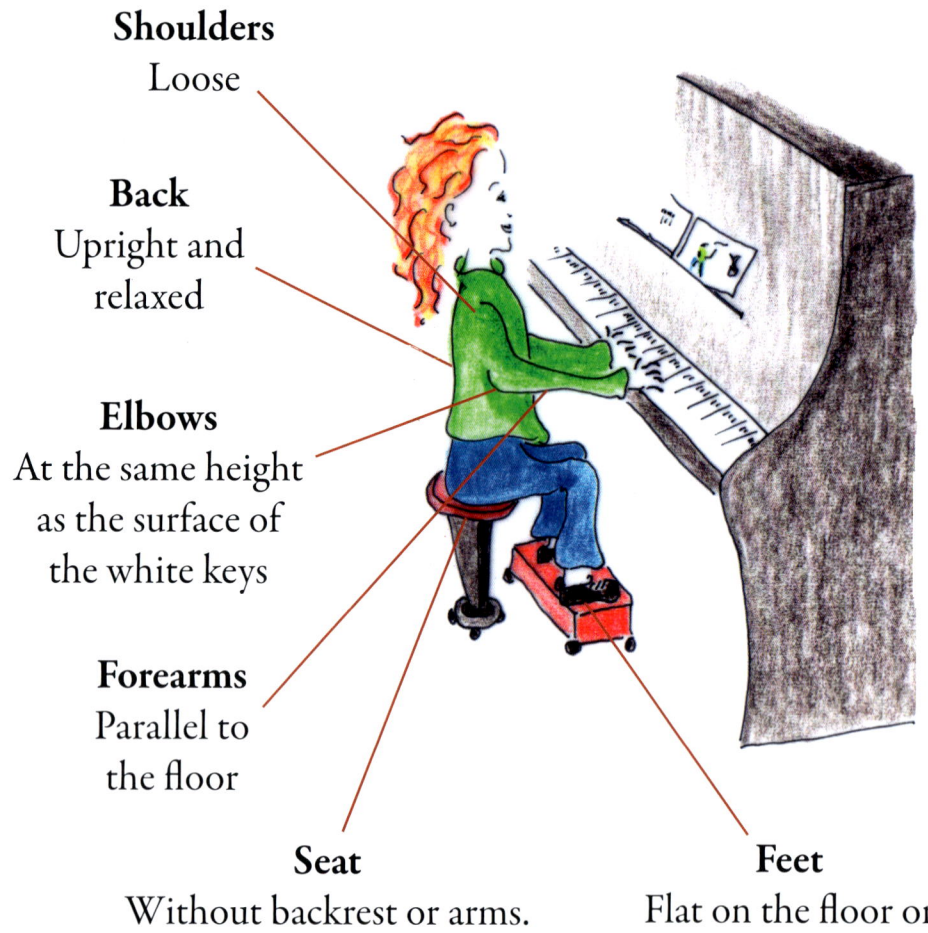

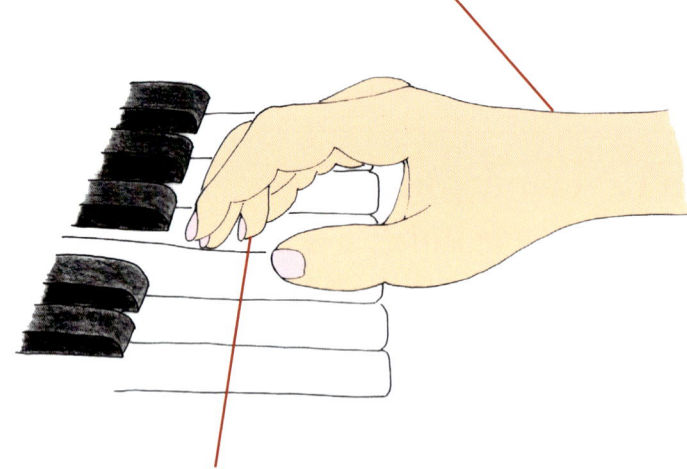

**Shoulders**
Loose

**Back**
Upright and relaxed

**Elbows**
At the same height as the surface of the white keys

**Forearms**
Parallel to the floor

**Seat**
Without backrest or arms. It should allow you to sit comfortably at the correct height for your **Elbows**

**Feet**
Flat on the floor or resting securely on a flat support (book/stool)

**Wrists**
Loose, and level with the back of your hands and forearms (not bent upwards or sagging down)

**Fingers and thumbs**
Imagine holding a large orange loosely in your hand. Your fingers are curved and rest always on the keys. Push keys with the sides of your thumbs

# Why No Notes?

Keyboard beginners want to do two things. They want to HAVE FUN playing familiar songs, melodies, riffs and grooves. And they want to MAKE PROGRESS developing foundation keyboard skills. Foundation keyboard skills include having a practical familiarity with the layout of a keyboard, learning to play using all fingers and thumbs, being able to play different patterns with each hand at the same time, reading music, playing with a beat, and playing musically (see *inside back cover*). Although beginners are often taught using standard music notation, it is easier, and more fun, to focus on foundation keyboard skills using tablature notation.

No Notes piano tablature shows where to put your hands, which fingers to use and when to play them. It is so very easy to understand that even absolute beginners can soon read No Notes music for themselves, and play favourite melodies, riffs and grooves, right from the start. No Notes pieces are such familiar favourites, beginners hardly realise that they are actually learning to 'find' their fingers (i.e. the fundamental keyboard skill of playing any finger or thumb at the correct moment, in a musical way). No Notes beginners also quickly build valuable confidence in their ability to read and play written music. And since No Notes music is based on standard notation, No Notes beginners are well prepared for standard notation in due course.

No Notes music is a simplified form of music notation designed to help absolute beginners bridge the gap between knowing nothing and having the ability to read and play standard music notation. No Notes music helps beginners develop confidence quickly in their ability to make both satisfying music and progress. No Notes graduates know from experience that learning challenging new musical skills is both possible and fun.

# Getting started

***No Notes Blues Primer* is a progressive course.** This means you start at the beginning and move on to the next step only once you have mastered the one you are on. You will learn faster if you listen a few times first to the riff, groove or scale you are tackling. Free recordings of the riffs, grooves and scales in this book are available from **www.NoNotes.co.uk**.

**First learn your finger numbers.** Lay one hand, palm downwards, on a piece of paper and draw around your fingers. Do the same for the other hand, then number the fingers 1, 2, 3, 4 and 5, starting with '1' for each thumb. Hold both hands in front of you, palms downwards with fingers extended, and ask a friend to touch different fingers at random. Practise to see how quickly you can say the finger number. Remember, your thumbs are both '1'.

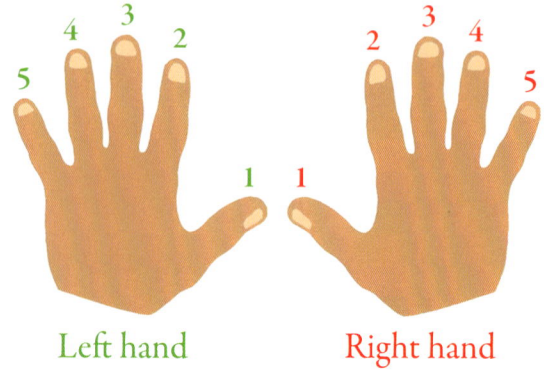

**Make sure your hands are in the right place.** The black keys on your keyboard are arranged in alternating groups of two and three. For each piece, a keyboard map shows which keys to play and which fingers to use. All 12-bar blues in this book use three hand positions.

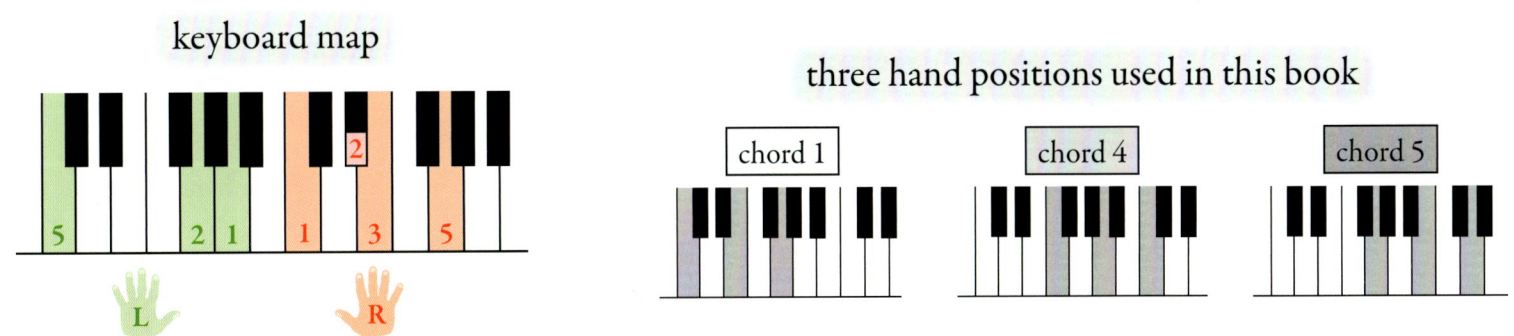

**Reading the music.** A song chart shows which fingers to play and when to play them. Notes for the **R**ight hand, are written in **R**ed above the line. Notes for the **L**eft hand, are written in **L**ime green below the line. Read song charts from left to right and push keys under the fingers indicated. A wider gap between two numbers means you wait longer before playing the second note. When two or more finger numbers are written on top of each other you push the keys at the same time, making a chord.

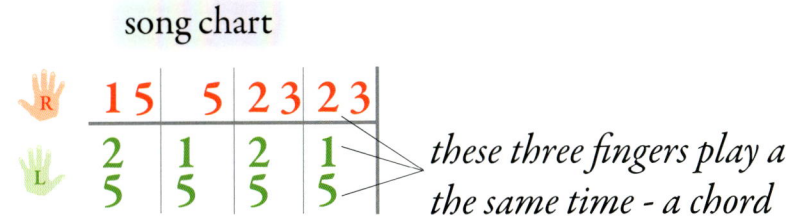

*these three fingers play at the same time - a chord*

# Practice hints

Learning to play the piano takes time. Make the most of your time at the keyboard by developing intelligent practising habits.

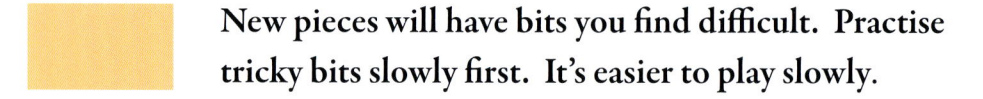

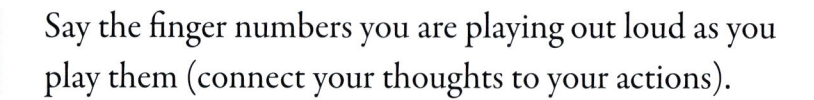

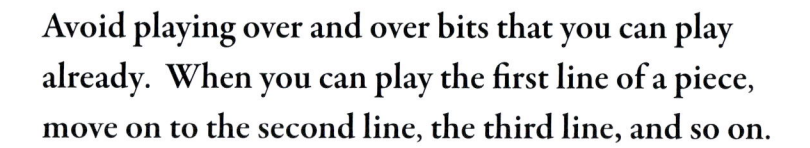

**New pieces will have bits you find difficult. Practise tricky bits slowly first. It's easier to play slowly.**

Say the finger numbers you are playing out loud as you play them (connect your thoughts to your actions).

**Avoid playing over and over bits that you can play already. When you can play the first line of a piece, move on to the second line, the third line, and so on.**

Playing different things in each hand at the same time is not easy. It can help first to play one hand and, instead of pushing keys, tap on your leg with your other hand, when it has notes to play. Remember to swap hands over.

**Aim to make your practice time interesting – work on several different things.**

Singing or humming phrases before you play them makes playing easier. Recordings of all No Notes music are freely available from **www.NoNotes.co.uk**.

**Keep time! Use a metronome, sometimes.**

Play No Notes music with a friend – it's half as hard and twice the fun! Sit side-by-side at the keyboard. The player on the left (as you face the keyboard) plays the right hand part. The player on the right plays the left hand part. Players' forearms will cross over each other.

**Try not to look at your fingers as you play. They will work without you watching!**

# Musical terms

| | |
|---:|:---|
| **backbeat** | 2nd and 4th beats of a 4-beat bar. |
| **bar** | Period of time defined by a given number of beats. All bars in *No Notes Blues Primer* are four beats long. |
| **beat** | A series of identically-spaced, short-duration stimuli perceived as points in time. Beats are generally specified in the range 40 to 240 beats per minute. A repetitive, regularly accented series of beats is a 'metre' or 'count'. |
| **chord** | Two or more notes played at the same time. |
| **groove** | Rhythmical accompaniment pattern (i.e. music supporting riffs and melodies). |
| **improvise** | Compose music as you are playing. |
| **metronome** | Device sounding a beat at variable speeds. |
| **notation** | Any system used to represent musical sounds by visual symbols. |
| **offbeat** | Played between beats. |
| **pitch** | The 'highness' or 'lowness' of a sound. Notes at the right-hand end of a keyboard are high. Notes at the left-hand end are low. |
| **rhythm** | Pattern of sound in time. |
| **riff** | Short, melodic phrase. |
| **straight 8s** | Rhythmic feel where a note between the beats is played precisely at the halfway point. |
| **swing** | Rhythmic feel where a note between the beats is played on roughly the final third of the beat. |
| **syncopation** | An unexpected emphasis (e.g. a weak beat is made strong). |
| **tapping a beat** | This is best done by resting the heel of your hand on your leg and tapping the beat lightly with your fingers. The tapping arm should be as relaxed as possible. |

# Step 1. Learning to walk

Place your hands like this ...

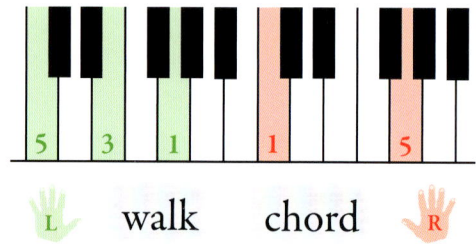

... and play this.

| chord R | 5<br>1 | 5<br>1 | 5<br>1 | 5<br>1 |
|---|---|---|---|---|
| walk L | 5 | 3 | 1 | 3 |

Now place your hands like this ...

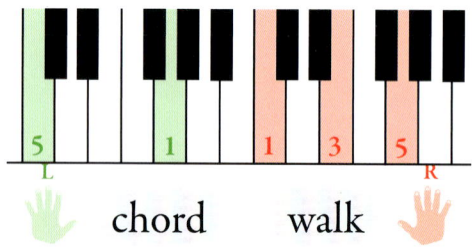

... and play this.

| walk R | 1 | 3 | 5 | 3 |
|---|---|---|---|---|
| chord L | 1<br>5 | 1<br>5 | 1<br>5 | 1<br>5 |

Practise these until you can play both versions comfortably, several times over, at a steady speed. It may help to play the 'walking' hand on its own first and add the chords incrementally: play just one chord and have three beats 'recovery time'; then play two chords and have two beats recovery time, and so on.

# Step 2. Shuffle Riff

Place your left hand here …

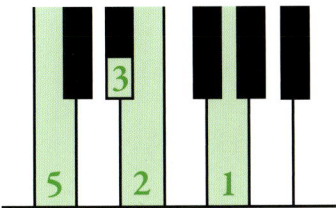

… and play this warm up pattern several times over.

L | 32 | 11 | 32 | 55 |

Place your right hand here …

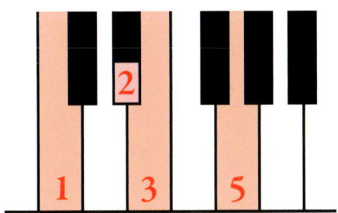

… and play this warm up pattern several times over.

R | 23 | 55 | 23 | 11 |

Now place your hands like this …

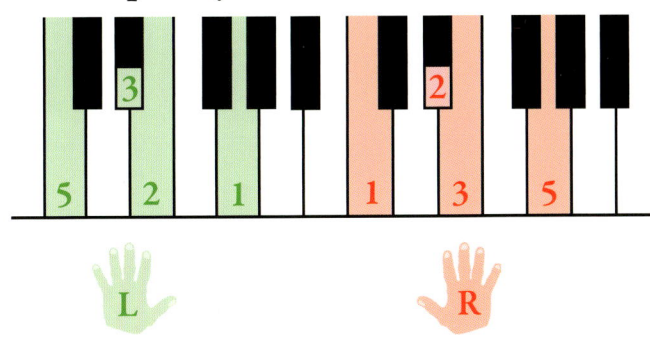

… and play Shuffle Riff with each hand separately, and then with both hands at the same time.

Shuffle Riff

R | 11 | 23 | 55 | 23 |
L | 55 | 32 | 11 | 32 |

# Step 3. Playing with a beat

Play Shuffle Riff with your right hand, saying, 'Yes – no – yes – no – ...' as you play each note.

| play R | 1 1 | 2 3 | 5 5 | 2 3 |
|---|---|---|---|---|
| say aloud | Yes No | Yes No | Yes No | Yes No |
| tap beat L | X | X | X | X |

Play Shuffle Riff with your left hand, saying, 'Yes – no – yes – no – ...' as you play each note.

| tap beat R | X | X | X | X |
|---|---|---|---|---|
| say aloud | Yes No | Yes No | Yes No | Yes No |
| play L | 5 5 | 3 2 | 1 1 | 3 2 |

As soon as you feel able, tap on your leg with your other hand every time you say 'yes'. Each 'yes' is a beat. There are four beats in the bar. Emphasise the first beat.

Play Shuffle Riff with one hand and a chord with the other (*right*). Play each version several times over without stopping. Keep a steady speed. It may help to play Shuffle Riff on its own first and add the chords incrementally (*see Step 1*).

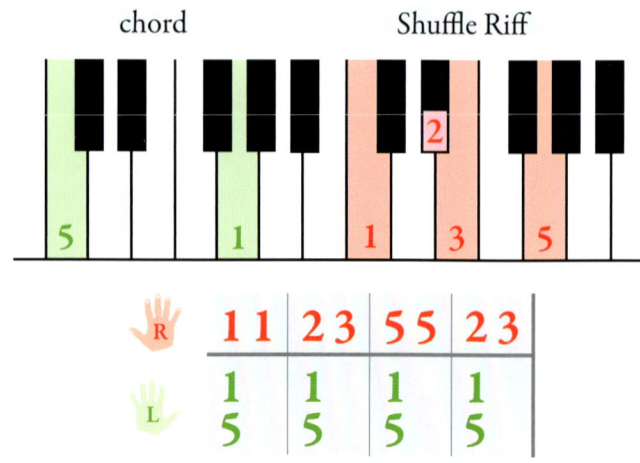

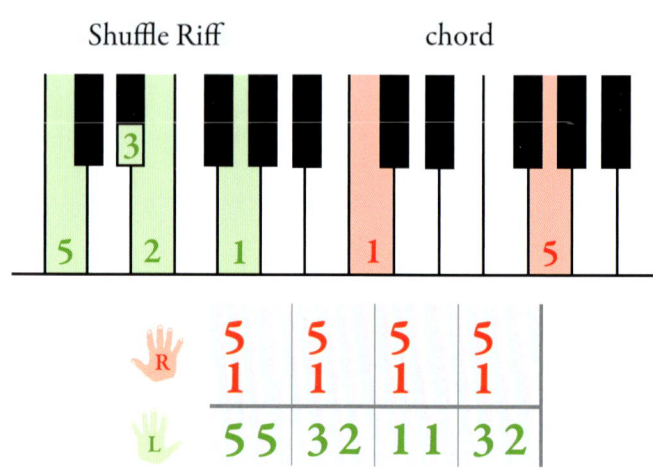

# Step 4. Backbeat Groove

Place your left hand here ...

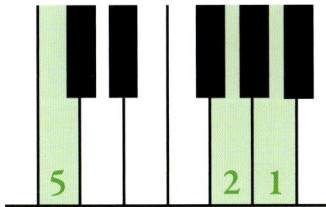

... and play Backbeat Groove. Emphasise chords on the 2nd and 4th beats – the 'back' beats (shaded darker grey in the song chart).

| 2 | 1 | 2 | 1 |
|---|---|---|---|
| 5 | 5 | 5 | 5 |

Place your right hand here ...

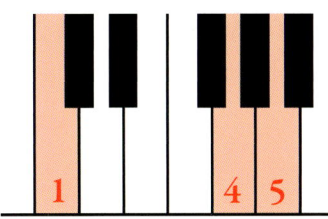

... and play Backbeat Groove. Emphasise chords on the 2nd and 4th beats – the 'back' beats (shaded darker grey in the song chart).

| 4 | 5 | 4 | 5 |
|---|---|---|---|
| 1 | 1 | 1 | 1 |

Play Backbeat Groove with one hand and Shuffle Riff with the other (*right*). Notice how chords on the back beats coincide with the black note in Shuffle Riff. Keep a steady speed. It may help to play Shuffle Riff on its own first and add the chords incrementally (*see Step 1*).

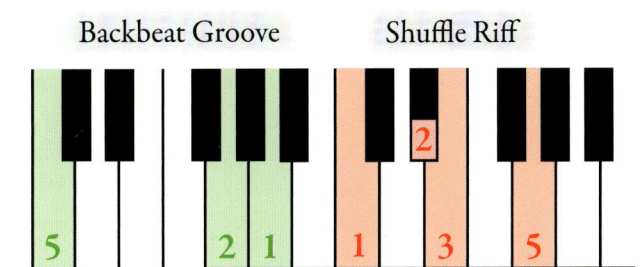

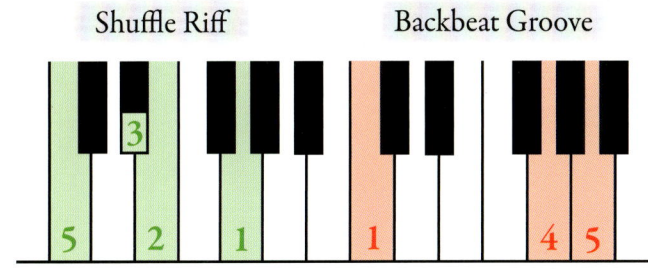

# Step 5. Chords 1, 4 and 5

Three hand positions are needed to play a simple 12-bar blues – **chord 1**, **chord 4** and **chord 5**.

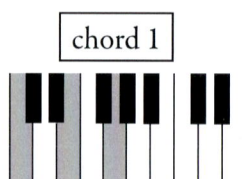 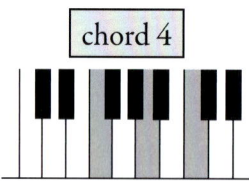 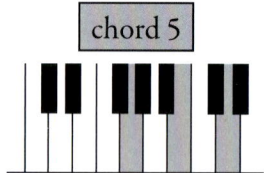

Play the 'walking' pattern, Shuffle Riff and Backbeat Groove in these three hand positions.

walking pattern

| R | 5 | 5 | 5 | 5 |
|---|---|---|---|---|
|   | 1 | 1 | 1 | 1 |
| L | 5 | 3 | 1 | 3 |

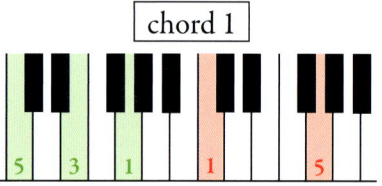 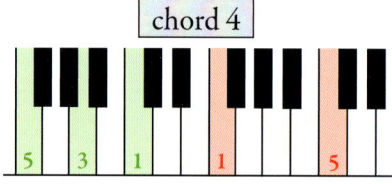 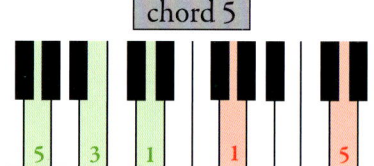

Shuffle Riff

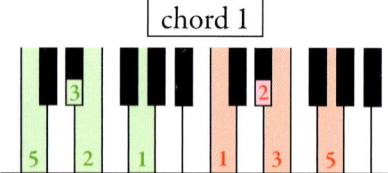 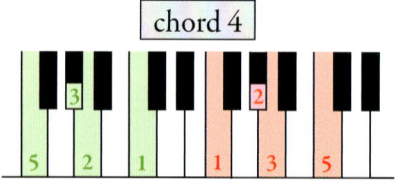 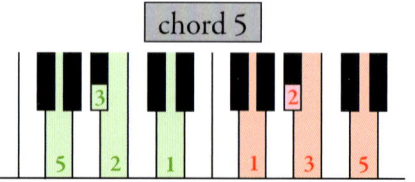

Backbeat Groove

| R | 4 | 5 | 4 | 5 |
|---|---|---|---|---|
|   | 1 | 1 | 1 | 1 |
| L | 2 | 1 | 2 | 1 |
|   | 5 | 5 | 5 | 5 |

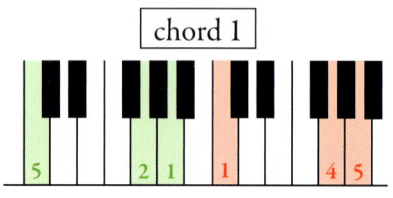 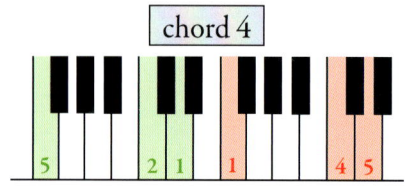 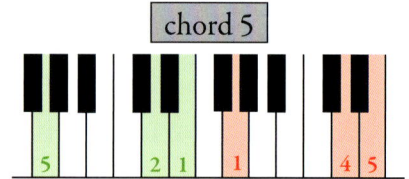

# Step 6. 12-bar blues

A 12-bar blues consists of three, 4-bar phrases. All 12-bar blues in
*No Notes Blues Primer* use chords 1, 4 and 5 (*see Step 5*) in this order:

| | | | | |
|---|---|---|---|---|
| 1st phrase | chord 1 | chord 1 | chord 1 | chord 1 |
| 2nd phrase | chord 4 | chord 4 | chord 1 | chord 1 |
| 3rd phrase | chord 5 | chord 4 | chord 1 | chord 1 |

Play a 12-bar blues with Shuffle Riff and Backbeat Groove. Don't forget to move both riff and groove to new hand positions at the same time. Remember as well to emphasise the 2nd and 4th beats of Backbeat Groove (shaded darker grey). Practise both versions shown below.

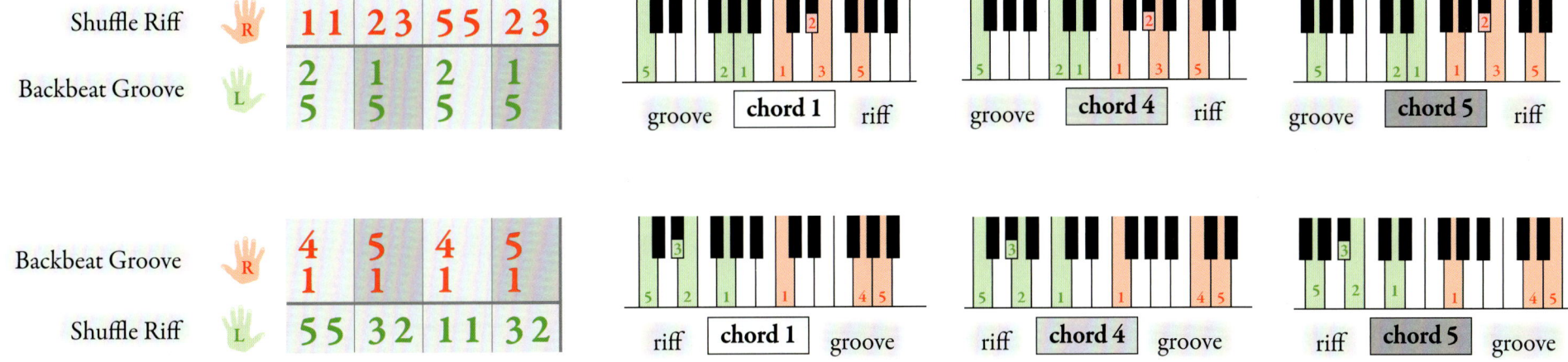

# Step 7. The blues scale

The blues scale is a series of six alternating white- and black-key notes, widely used for improvising (*below*). Play the blues scale using the thumb (1) for all white-key notes, and the middle finger (3) for all black-key notes (fingering is the same for both hands). Play the top note once only.

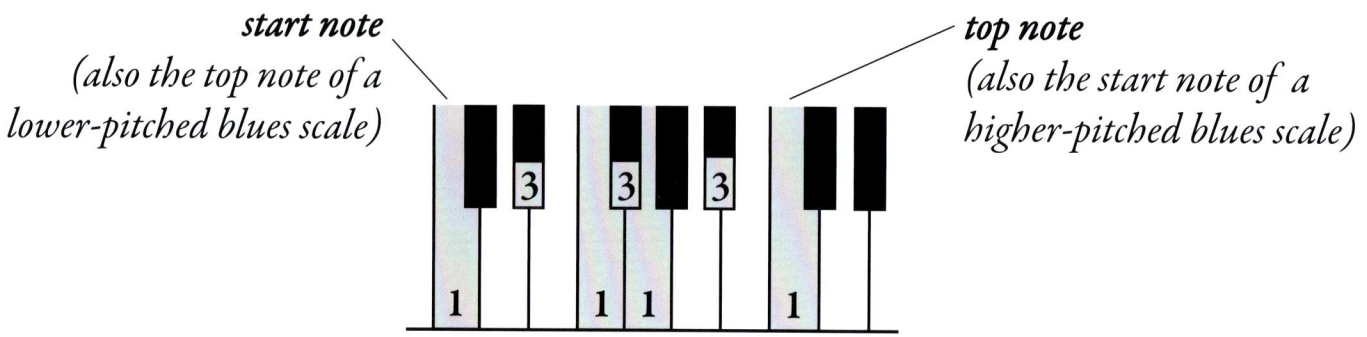

Practise the blues scale up and down, saying, 'Yes – no – yes – no – ...' as you play each note and tapping each beat ('yes') on your leg with your other hand (*below*). Notice that one play-through of the blues scale is two bars long, and also that the final note lasts for two beats.

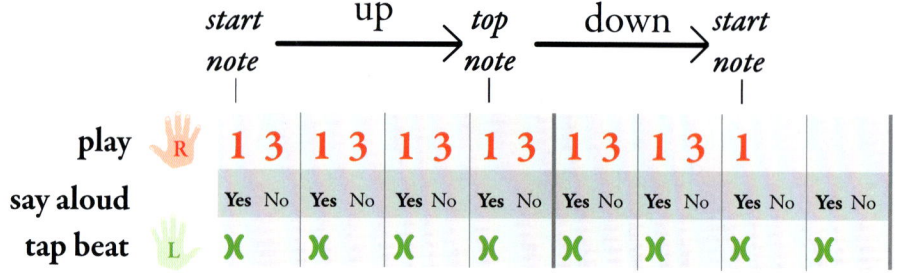

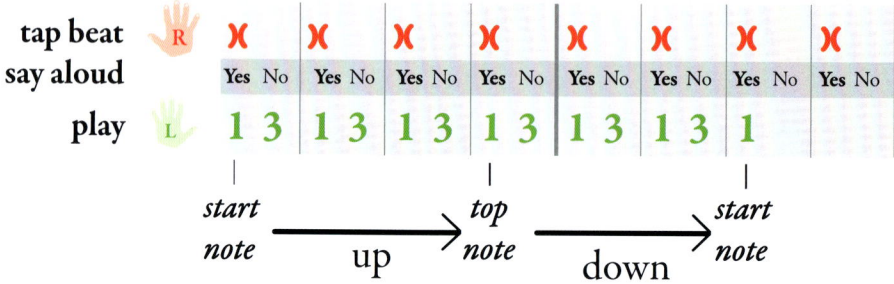

# Step 8. Using the blues scale – 'inversions'

Scales do not have to begin on their lowest note or end on their top note. The keyboard maps below show one complete version ('inversion') of the blues scale starting on each note of the scale in turn.

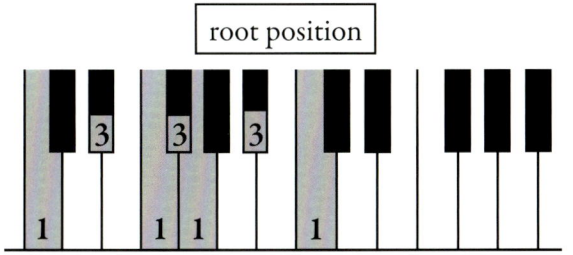
root position

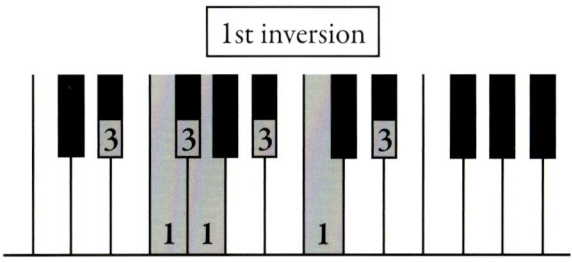
1st inversion

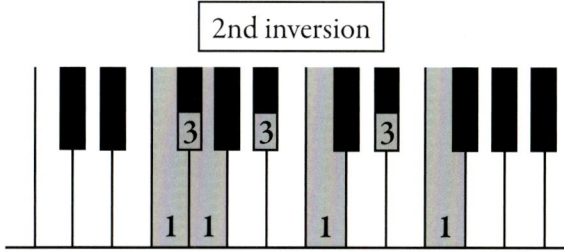
2nd inversion

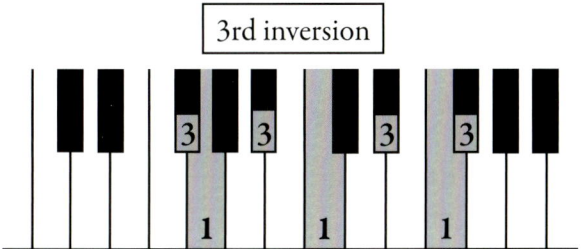
3rd inversion

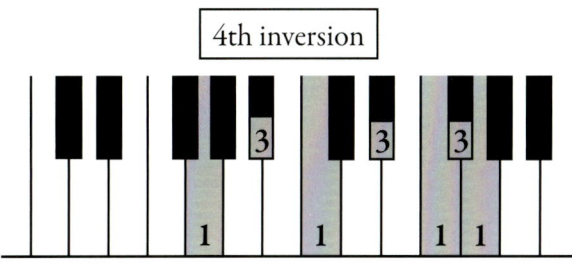
4th inversion

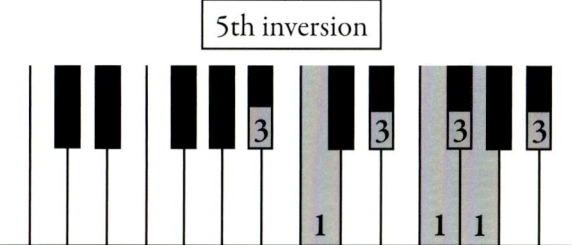
5th inversion

Play each inversion of the scale, up and down, with each hand separately.
Notice that the 1st, 3rd and 5th inversions begin with the middle finger on a black note.
Remember to play the top note of each inversion once only. Tap a beat as you play (*see Step 7*).

# Step 9. Blues Scale Blues

In this blues the right hand plays each inversion of the blues scale once (up and down), and the left hand plays Backbeat Groove.

The notes for each inversion of the scale are shown by miniature keyboard maps above the right-hand part. Remember, the top note of each inversion is played once only, and the final note of each inversion lasts for two beats.

Backbeat Groove uses the 12-bar blues chord sequence (see *Step 6*). Remember to emphasise the 2nd and 4th beats of Backbeat Groove (shaded darker grey).

When you can play this blues, practise with the scale in the left hand and the groove in the right.

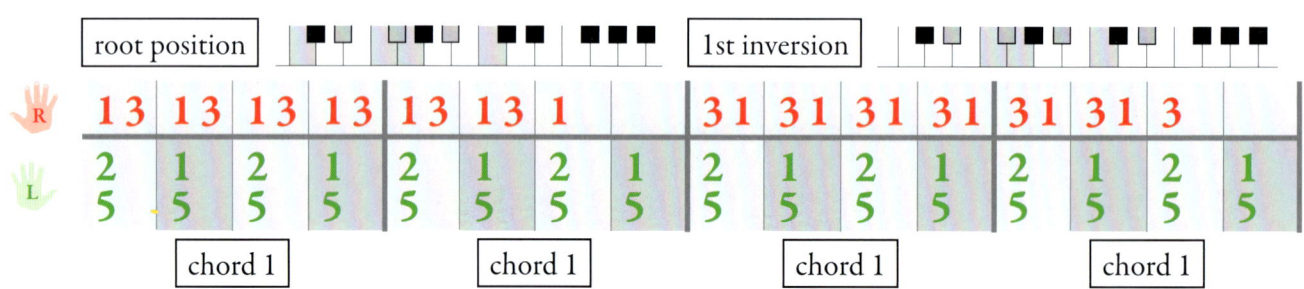

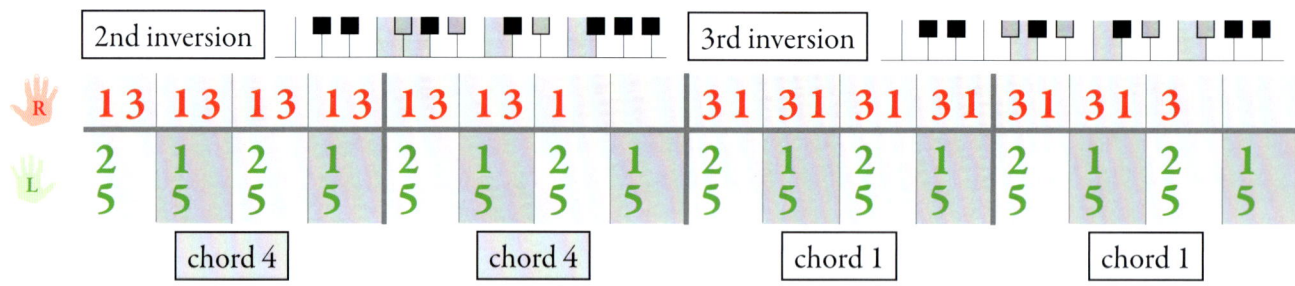

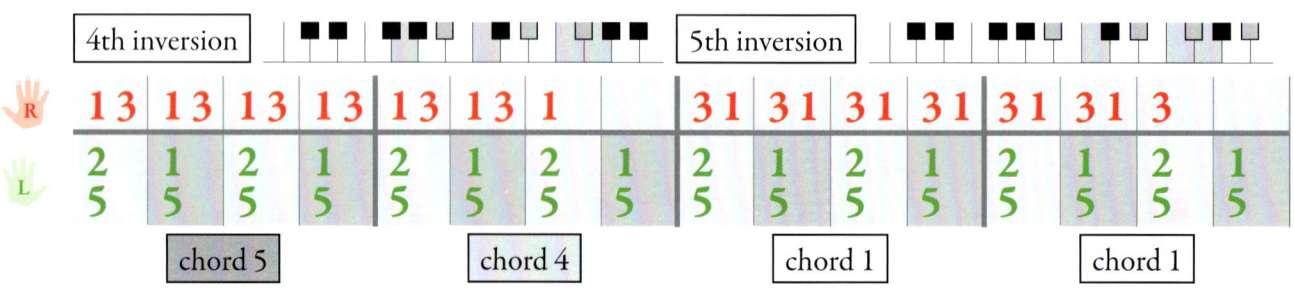

# Step 10. Syncopated Rhythm

Syncopation occurs when there is an unexpected emphasis (e.g. a weak beat is made strong). Clap Syncopated Rhythm (*below*). Take care to count out loud at a steady speed and emphasise the two offbeat claps.

| count aloud | 1 | + | 2 | + | 3 | + | 4 | + | 1 | + | 2 | + | 3 | + | 4 | + |
|---|---|---|---|---|---|---|---|---|---|---|---|---|---|---|---|---|
| clap rhythm | X | | X | | X | | X | X | X | | X | | X | | X | |

*It can help at first to say, 'and' ('+'), between each beat. As soon as you can, try to say only the numbers (i.e. no 'ands').*

Count out loud, tapping Syncopated Rhythm (shaded darker grey) with one hand, and a beat with the other.

| count aloud | 1 | 2 | 3 | 4 | + | 1 | + | 2 | 3 | 4 |
|---|---|---|---|---|---|---|---|---|---|---|
| tap rhythm (R) | X | X | X | X | X | X | X | X | X | X |
| tap beat (L) | X | X | X | X | | X | | X | X | X |

| count aloud | 1 | 2 | 3 | 4 | + | 1 | + | 2 | 3 | 4 |
|---|---|---|---|---|---|---|---|---|---|---|
| tap beat (R) | X | X | X | X | | X | | X | X | X |
| tap rhythm (L) | X | X | X | X | X | X | X | X | X | X |

Pass Syncopated Rhythm (shaded darker grey) between your hands several times over without a break. Make sure your counting does not get faster or slower. When you count aloud try not to say 'ands'.

| count aloud | 1 | 2 | 3 | 4 | + | 1 | + | 2 | 3 | 4 | 1 | 2 | 3 | 4 | + | 1 | + | 2 | 3 | 4 |
|---|---|---|---|---|---|---|---|---|---|---|---|---|---|---|---|---|---|---|---|---|
| tap (R) | X | X | X | X | X | X | X | X | X | X | X | X | X | X | X | X | X | X | X | X |
| tap (L) | X | X | X | X | X | X | X | X | X | X | X | X | X | X | X | X | X | X | X | X |

# Step 11. Syncopated Groove

Play these notes with your left hand (notice the thumb plays three different keys – **1”, 1’ and 1)** …

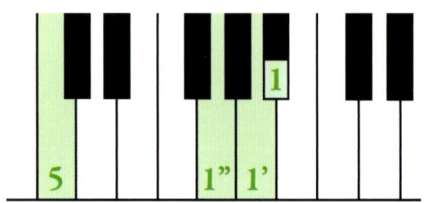

… to make three chords in this order.

| L | | | |
|---|---|---|---|
| 1”<br>5 | 1’<br>5 | 1<br>5 | 1’<br>5 |

Play these notes with your right hand (notice the little finger plays three different keys – **5”, 5’ and 5)** …

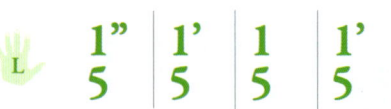

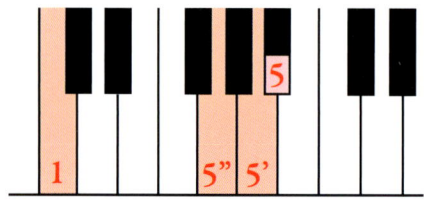

… to make three chords in this order.

| R | | | |
|---|---|---|---|
| 5”<br>1 | 5’<br>1 | 5<br>1 | 5’<br>1 |

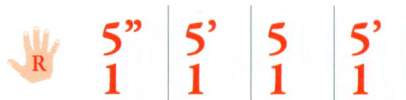

Use these chords to play Syncopated Groove (*below*). One hand plays the chords on the beat and the other plays them using Syncopated Rhythm (shaded darker grey, *see Step10*). Practise both versions shown below.

| | | | | | | | | | |
|---|---|---|---|---|---|---|---|---|---|
| **Syncopated Rhythm** | R | 5”<br>1 | 5’<br>1 | 5<br>1 | 5’ 5”<br>1 1 | 5”<br>1 | 5’<br>1 | 5<br>1 | 5’<br>1 |
| **on the beat** | L | 1”<br>5 | 1’<br>5 | 1<br>5 | 1’<br>5 | 1”<br>5 | 1’<br>5 | 1<br>5 | 1’<br>5 |

| | | | | | | | | | |
|---|---|---|---|---|---|---|---|---|---|
| **on the beat** | R | 5”<br>1 | 5’<br>1 | 5<br>1 | 5’<br>1 | 5”<br>1 | 5’<br>1 | 5<br>1 | 5’<br>1 |
| **Syncopated Rhythm** | L | 1”<br>5 | 1’<br>5 | 1<br>5 | 1’ 1”<br>5 5 | 1”<br>5 | 1’<br>5 | 1<br>5 | 1’<br>5 |

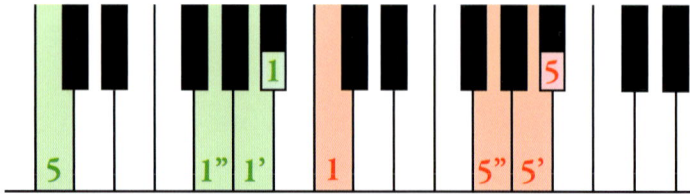

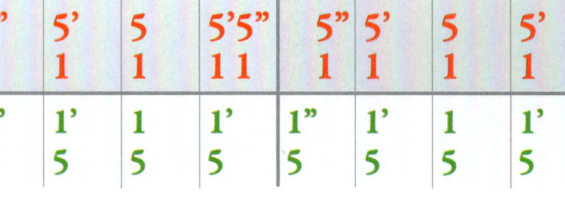

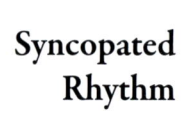

# Step 12. Syncopated Groove Blues

Play Syncopated Groove (*see Step 11*) in the three hand positions of a 12-bar blues.

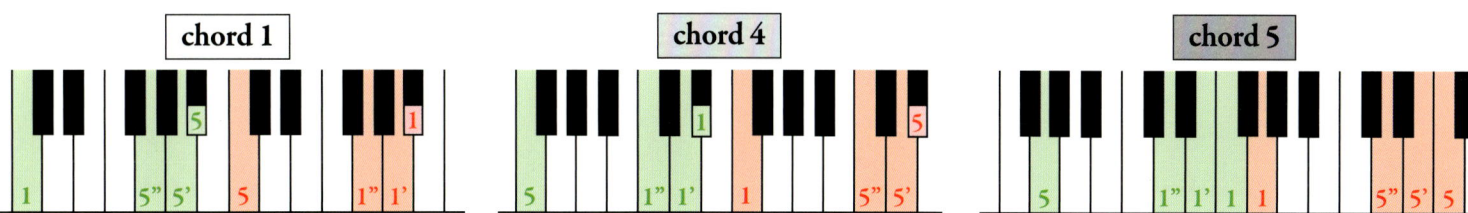

In Syncopated Groove Blues (*right*) Syncopated Rhythm (shaded darker grey, *see Step 10*) passes from one hand to the other every two bars.

| | chord 1 | | | | chord 1 | | | | chord 1 | | | | chord 1 | | | |
|---|---|---|---|---|---|---|---|---|---|---|---|---|---|---|---|---|
| R | 5” 1 | 5’ 1 | 5 1 | 5’5” 1 1 | 5” 1 | 5’ 1 | 5 1 | 5’ 1 | 5” 1 | 5’ 1 | 5 1 | 5’ 1 | 5” 1 | 5’ 1 | 5 1 | 5’ 1 |
| L | 1” 5 | 1’ 5 | 1 5 | 1’ 5 | 1” 5 | 1’ 5 | 1 5 | 1’ 5 | 1” 5 | 1’ 5 | 1 5 | 1’1” 5 5 | 1” 5 | 1’ 5 | 1 5 | 1’ 5 |

| | chord 4 | | | | chord 4 | | | | chord 1 | | | | chord 1 | | | |
|---|---|---|---|---|---|---|---|---|---|---|---|---|---|---|---|---|
| R | 5” 1 | 5’ 1 | 5 1 | 5’5” 1 1 | 5” 1 | 5’ 1 | 5 1 | 5’ 1 | 5” 1 | 5’ 1 | 5 1 | 5’ 1 | 5” 1 | 5’ 1 | 5 1 | 5’ 1 |
| L | 1” 5 | 1’ 5 | 1 5 | 1’ 5 | 1” 5 | 1’ 5 | 1 5 | 1’ 5 | 1” 5 | 1’ 5 | 1 5 | 1’1” 5 5 | 1” 5 | 1’ 5 | 1 5 | 1’ 5 |

| | chord 5 | | | | ✱ chord 4 | | | | chord 1 | | | | chord 1 | | | |
|---|---|---|---|---|---|---|---|---|---|---|---|---|---|---|---|---|
| R | 5” 1 | 5’ 1 | 5 1 | 5’5”✱ 1 1 | 5” 1 | 5’ 1 | 5 1 | 5’ 1 | 5” 1 | 5’ 1 | 5 1 | 5’ 1 | 5” 1 | 5’ 1 | 5 1 | 5’ 1 |
| L | 1” 5 | 1’ 5 | 1 5 | 1’ 5 | 1” 5 | 1’ 5 | 1 5 | 1’ 5 | 1” 5 | 1’ 5 | 1 5 | 1’1” 5 5 | 1” 5 | 1’ 5 | 1 5 | 1’ 5 |

✱ Play this chord in the chord 4 position.

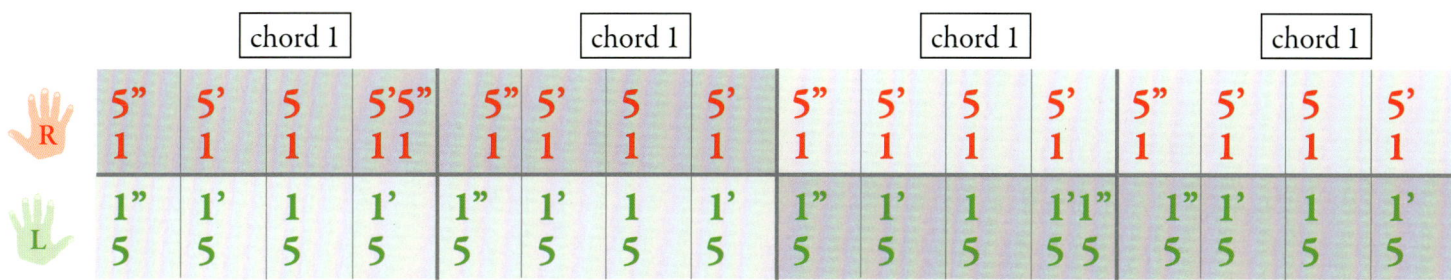

# Step 13. Syncopated Riff

Count aloud at a steady speed and clap this rhythm (*right*).

| count aloud | 1 | + | 2 | + | 3 | + | 4 | + |
|---|---|---|---|---|---|---|---|---|
| clap | X | X |  | X | X | X | X | X |

It can help at first to say, 'and' ('+'), between each beat. As soon as you can, try to say only the numbers (i.e. no 'ands').

Use this rhythm to play Syncopated Riff (*right*) with each hand separately. Tap a beat with the other hand.

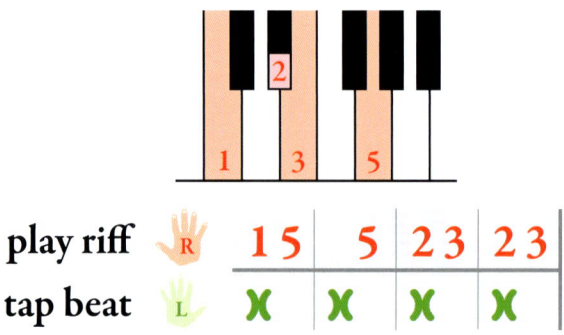

| play riff (R) | 1 5 | 5 | 2 3 | 2 3 |
|---|---|---|---|---|
| tap beat (L) | X | X | X | X |

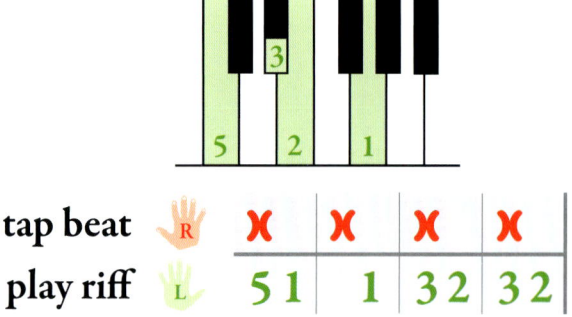

| tap beat (R) | X | X | X | X |
|---|---|---|---|---|
| play riff (L) | 5 1 | 1 | 3 2 | 3 2 |

Make a 12-bar blues with Syncopated Riff with Backbeat Groove (*see Steps 5 and 6*). It may help to play Syncopated Riff on its own first and add the chords incrementally (*see Step 1*). Remember to emphasise the 2nd and 4th beats of Backbeat Groove (shaded darker grey).

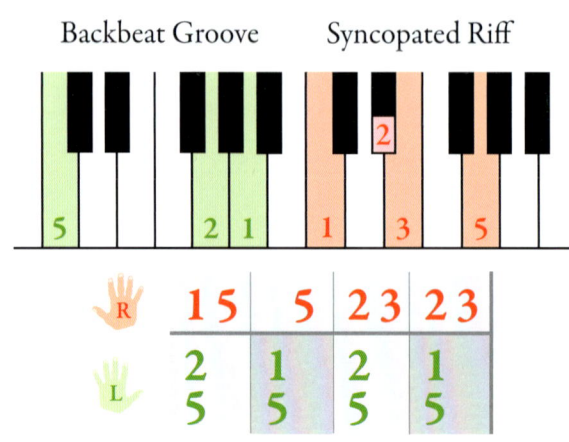

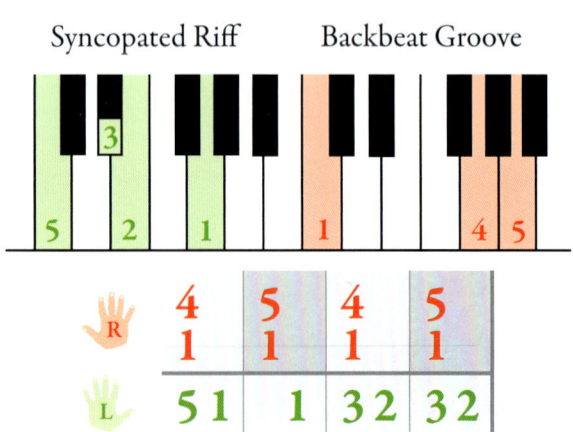

# Step 14. Turnarounds

A 12-bar blues is often played several times over. Repetition allows a song to tell a story, or an instrumentalist to develop an improvisation. When a 12-bar blues is repeated, the chords near the end of the blues are often changed – to emphasise the end of each 12-bar section and also to create a sense of anticipation for the next 12-bar section. This chord change is called a turnaround.

A very simple and familiar turnaround involves changing the chord in bar 12 from chord 1 (*see Step 6*) to chord 5 (*below*).

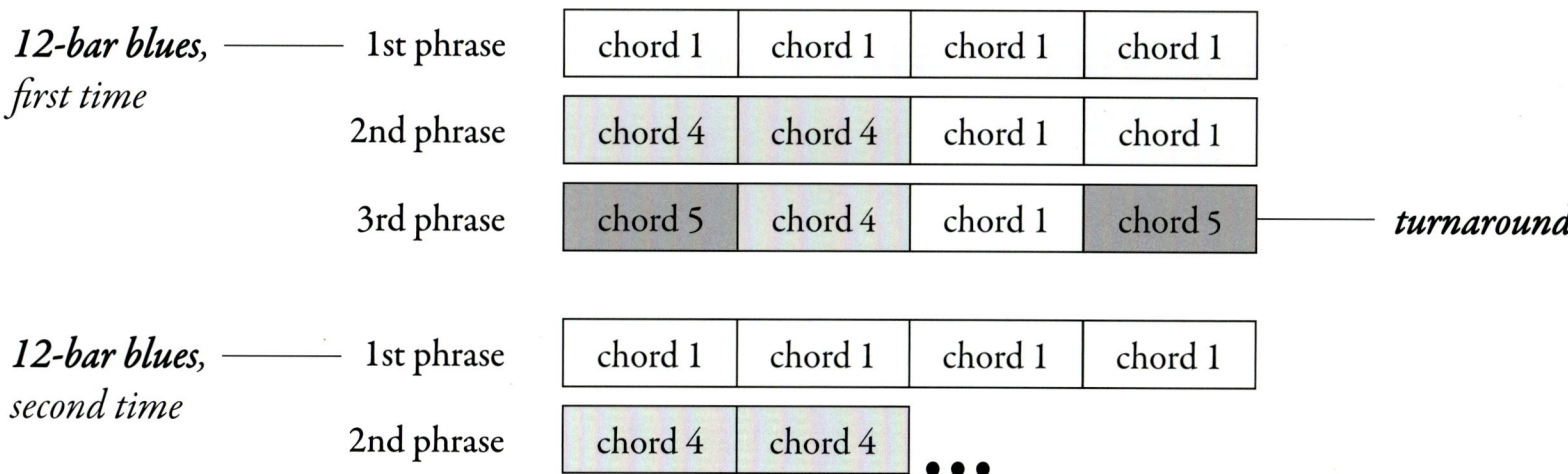

Practise changing the chord in bar 12 from chord 1 to chord 5 in the various 12-bar blues you have learned so far. Probably, you will want to modify the riff you are playing as well, to make it 'fit' the changed chord.

# Step 15. Straight 8s and swing

Music can be played with a straight 8s or a swing 'feel'. The difference is in the timing of notes **between** the beats. In straight 8s, notes between beats are played precisely at the halfway point. '**Thir**-teen **four**-teen **fif**-teen **six**-teen', has a straight 8s feel when spoken naturally. Practise straight 8s rhythms by saying, 'and', for notes between each beat – '**1**-and-**2**-and-**3**-and-**4**-and'.

In swing, a note played on the beat lasts longer than a note played between the beats. Notes between beats are played on roughly the final third of the beat. '**Thir**-ty **for**-ty **fif**-ty **six**-ty', has a swing feel when spoken fast and naturally. A run of swing half-beat notes has a 'limping' or 'galloping' quality (depending on the speed!). Practise swing rhythms by saying, 'doo', for notes on the beat and, 'bi', for notes between beats. Be careful to say (and play), 'doo, bi-doo, bi-doo, bi-doo, bi-', (i.e. long, short-long, short-long, short-long, short-) and not, 'doo-bi, doo-bi, doo-bi, doo-bi'.

All music in *No Notes Blues Primer* has been presented in straight 8s. Look again at each step and play the riffs and grooves with a swing feel. Two examples are shown here (*right*). Notice how, in swing, notes between beats ('bi') are closer to the *following* beat than to the preceding beat.

| say aloud | doo | bi | doo | bi | doo | bi | doo | bi | doo | bi | doo | bi | doo | bi | doo | bi |
|---|---|---|---|---|---|---|---|---|---|---|---|---|---|---|---|---|
| tap beat | X | | X | | X | | X | | X | | X | | X | | X | |

Shuffle Riff (Step 2)

| R | 1 | 1 | 2 | 3 | 5 | 5 | 2 | 3 | 1 | 1 | 2 | 3 | 5 | 5 | 2 | 3 |
| L | 5 | 5 | 3 | 2 | 1 | 1 | 3 | 2 | 5 | 5 | 3 | 2 | 1 | 1 | 3 | 2 |

Syncopated Groove (Step 11)

| R | 5" / 1 | | 5' / 1 | | 5 / 1 | | 5' / 1 | 5" / 1 | | 5" / 1 | 5' / 1 | | 5 / 1 | | 5' / 1 | |
| L | 1" / 5 | | 1' / 5 | | 1 / 5 | | 1' / 5 | | 1" / 5 | | 1' / 5 | | 1 / 5 | | 1' / 5 | |

# Step 16. Playing the blues

Have a go at making up your own blues. Start by recombining riffs and grooves presented in *No Notes Blues Primer* – for example Shuffle Riff and Syncopated Groove, or the blues scale with Syncopated Riff. Try changing pitches, rhythms and also *where* in the bar you *start* to play a riff. Listen carefully to your mistakes. Often these can be the start of something good. When you have ideas you like, remember to experiment with both straight 8s and swing feels, and also to play your ideas in all three 12-bar blues hand positions. A few more bluesy patterns are shown below.

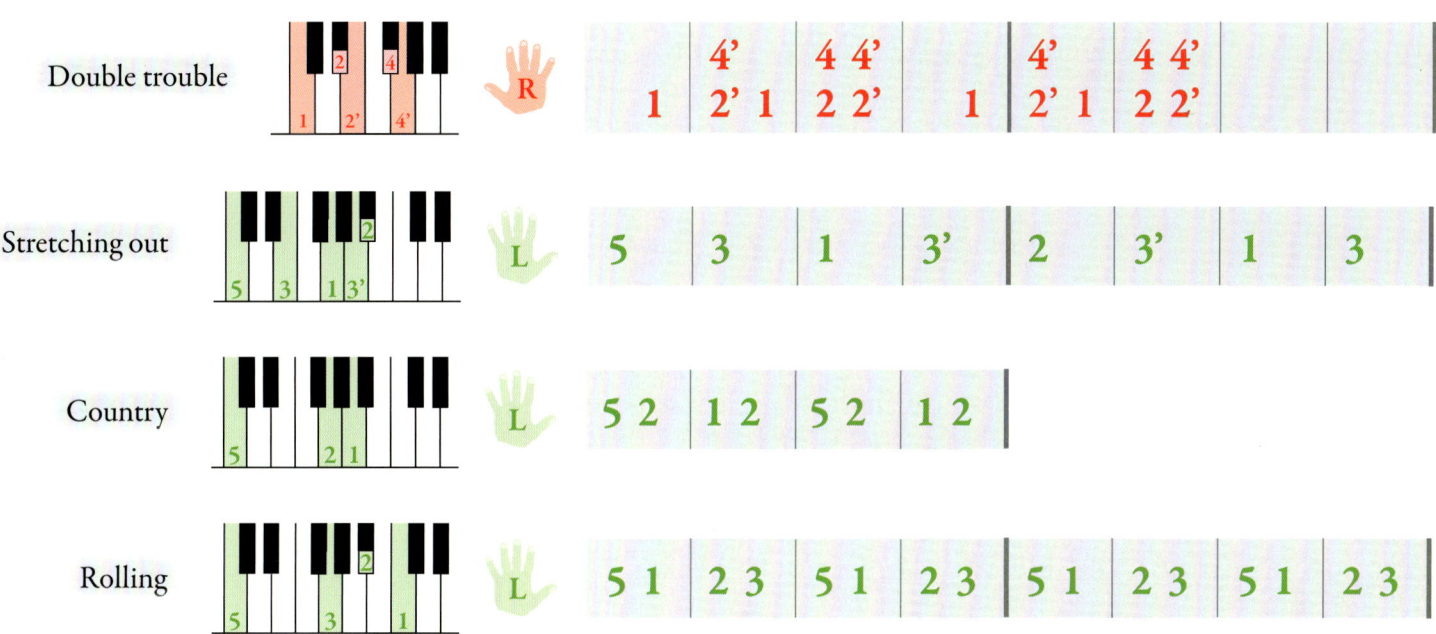

When you play a 12-bar blues imagine you are telling a story. Ask musical 'questions', give musical 'answers', and always leave space – thinking time – between your musical ideas. Listen to other musicians. Play with other musicians. Imitate what you like. Have fun!

# Acknowledgements

I've had so much help and encouragement developing No Notes.

My students over the years have shown me, time and again, the value of simple and attractive teaching materials.

My family, friends and colleagues too have made many comments and suggestions, especially Lizzie Higginson, Ben Lloyd, Sarah Lloyd, Judy Lloyd, Anne Michèle de Deus Silva, Bernardita Muñoz Chereau and Kate Miller. Lastly, I'm very grateful to Russ Davidson, Oliver Marler, Nadia Sheltawy and Andy Moss for invaluable technical and creative support. Thank you all!

*No Notes Blues Primer* is published with funds raised by a Kickstarter campaign (March–April 2015).

Kickstarter backers whose generosity has made this publication possible include Vincent Lloyd-Bonney, Russ Button, Simon Higginson, Ben Lloyd, Sarah Lloyd, Marlon Lloyd Malcolm, Ali Maskell, Sally Odd, Fanny Prior, Joseph Raine, Andrew Wilson, Kenneth Wilson, John Zealley and Kirsty Zealley.

**In loving memory of Monica Margaret and William Harry**